ENTS

THIS BOOK OFFERS SOME
TANTALIZING GLIMPSES OF
NORWEGIAN NATURE.
FROM COASTS AND MOUNTAINS.
FROM BUSTLING CITIES AND
UNSPOILT WILDERNESS.

THIS IS NORWAY

ICY MOUNTAINS AND WARM-HEARTED PEOPLE. DEEP FJORDS CARVED INTO THE BEDROCK. FERTILE VALLEYS, ENCHANTING VILLAGES AND CASCADING RIVERS. GLACIERS LIKE GLISTENING WISPS OF CREAM ON UNSPOILT LANDSCAPES. A COUNTRY OF CONTRASTS AND DRAMA. THE MIDNIGHT SUN, THE BUSTLING OSLO STREETS, THE DARK SEASON, THE COASTAL STEAMER, NIDAROS CATHEDRAL, IDYLLIC MEADOWS BURSTING WITH FLOWERS, AND THE DANGEROUS POLAR BEARS OF SVALBARD. WARM SUMMER DAYS, STORMY SEAS, 50 DEGREES BELOW ZERO, AND A NATION THAT HAS LEARNED TO ADAPT TO THE FORCES OF NATURE. THIS IS NORWAY.

Left: Fruit trees in blossom, Hardanger.
Above: Norwegian fjord horse.

HISTORY, CULTURE AND TRADITION

HISTORY

Norway - "the way to the north" - is an appropriate name for the most northerly country in Europe. With its 387,000 km², Norway is Europe's fifth largest country, although its population is only 4.5 million. Norway borders Sweden, Finland and Russia in the east, and the Atlantic Ocean in the west. Archeological discoveries indicate that Norway's first inhabitants settled here at the end of the last Ice Age, about 11,000 years ago. Initially, Norwegians depended on fishing and trapping for their livelihood. Later, they developed ocean-going ships, and became expert seafarers. Military expansion and flourishing cultural development characterized the Viking period (800-1050). King Harald Hårfagre unified Norway as one kingdom just before 900. The Viking kings Olav Tryggvason and St Olav introduced Christianity in about 1000. In the High Middle Ages, the "Norges-veldet" (Norwegian dominion) was a major North European power, and included Iceland, Greenland, the Faroe Islands and parts of Sweden. Norway was united with Denmark from 1380 to 1814, and with Sweden from 1814 until 1905, when it finally regained its independence.

The 5000-year-old rock carvings from Alta are listed as a Unesco World Heritage Site.

The statue of St Olav at Stiklestad.

The Oseberg ship, AD 834.

THE ROYAL FAMILY

Norway is a constitutional monarchy. The King is the head of state, but has no real political power. Among the people of Norway, however, the royal family has always had a special role as a symbol of the country's independence. Since 1905, the country has had three kings: Haakon VII, Olav V, and the current monarch, Harald V.

Left: The Royal Palace.
Above: The royal family on the palace balcony.

Left: The opening of the Storting (parliament).
Below: The Storting.

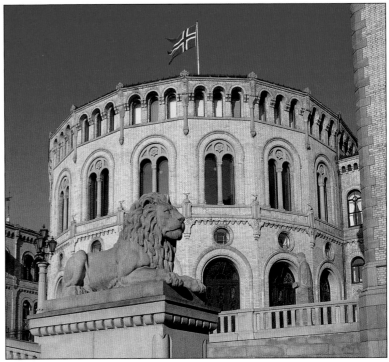

DEMOCRACY

Today, Norway is a well-developed democracy with comprehensive welfare systems. The country is governed according to parliamentary principles, where the Storting (parliament) has legislative power and the government has executive power.
The Riksforsamling (National Assembly) drew up Norway's constitution at Eidsvoll in 1814.

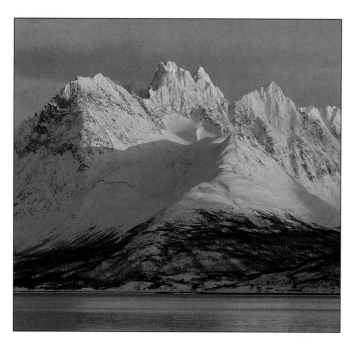

Roald Amundsen (1872-1928) was an important polar explorer, and led many challenging expeditions. He was the first person to reach the South Pole, where he planted the Norwegian flag on 14 December 1911.

Roald Amundsen

ADVENTURERS WHO OVERCAME BARRIERS

Fridtjof Nansen (1861-1930) was a renowned polar explorer, scientist, politician and humanist. He crossed Greenland on skis in 1888, and from 1893 to 1896 he undertook an epic expedition through the ice of the Arctic Ocean on the polar vessel "Fram". In 1922 Nansen received the Nobel Peace Prize for his humanitarian work.

Fridtjof Nansen

Thor Heyerdahl (born in 1914) is the most famous explorer of our time. On his balsa raft, the Kon-Tiki, he allowed the currents to float him from Peru in South America to Polynesia in the Pacific, to prove that the Polynesians could have originated in South America. In the same way, he used the papyrus raft Ra II to prove that people could have crossed the Atlantic in ancient times.

Right: Thor Heyerdahl on Easter Island.

WORLD-FAMOUS NORWEGIAN ARTISTS

Three Norwegian writers have received the Nobel Prize in literature: Bjørnstjerne Bjørnson (1832-1910), Knut Hamsun (1859-1952) and Sigrid Undset (1882-1949).

But one of the world's most important dramatists never received this honour. Henrik Ibsen (1828-1906) enriched European theatre with psychological depth and masterly stagecraft. Ibsen's plays are still performed at the world's most famous theatres, and literature researchers regularly publish new books interpreting the dramatist and his plays. "A Doll's House" and "The Wild Duck" are among his finest works. "Peer Gynt" is also well known, especially because of the music that Edvard Grieg composed for this play.

Henrik Ibsen

Edvard Munch (1863-1944) was a pioneer in the art of painting. He wanted to express the innermost feelings of human beings. He painted melancholy and angst, but also the joy of living and love.
Above: "The Girls on the Bridge", oil painting by Edvard Munch.

Edvard Grieg (1843-1907) put Norway on the international music map with his sparkling and vital music. A fresh breath of Norwegian nature inspires his work. When you listen to his music, you can visualize the fruit trees blossoming in Hardanger, waterfalls, fjords and mountains. Today Troldhaugen – Edvard Grieg's home, near Bergen – is a popular museum.

Edvard Grieg

11

NORWEGIAN NATIONAL DRESS

There is growing interest in the traditional, beautiful and colourful Norwegian national dress, or bunad. The costumes are a very popular choice for special occasions such as weddings, baptisms, confirmations, and the National Day. Norway has a wealth of national costumes.

Each region has developed its own distinctive design. The bunad is often richly decorated with embroidery and silver jewellery. Traditionally, a man wears a magnificent ornamented knife with his bunad.

Above left: "Hardingfele" (Norwegian fiddle).
Above right: Knives from Telemark.
Below: National costumes from Jølster in Sunnfjord.

12

STAVE CHURCHES - A MEDIEVAL HERITAGE IN WOOD

The stave churches are unique and irreplaceable relics of a bygone age. Unesco has designated the stave church of Urnes in Sogn as a World Heritage Site. Historians estimate that Norway once had about a thousand stave churches. Today, only 28 remain. Preserving the stave churches is a high priority for Norwegian conservation authorities. The most famous are the Borgund and Urnes stave churches in Sogn, which both date from about 1150, and Heddal stave church in Telemark, dating from about 1250. For the traveller of today, the stave churches are fascinating and exotic vestiges of a remote medieval era.

Above: Heddal stave church.
Right: Detail from Urnes stave church.

Above: Norwegian salmon - a tempting culinary delicacy.

Left: The fishing grounds outside Lofoten.

Below: Drying fish on racks in Lofoten. Dried Lofoten cod has been exported to many countries in Europe since Viking times.

Above right: Norwegian mountain farm in Sogn.
Below right: Rømmegrøt (sour-cream porridge), fenalår (cured mutton) and flatbrød (thin wafer crispbread).

Below, far right: Tempting Norwegian specialties.

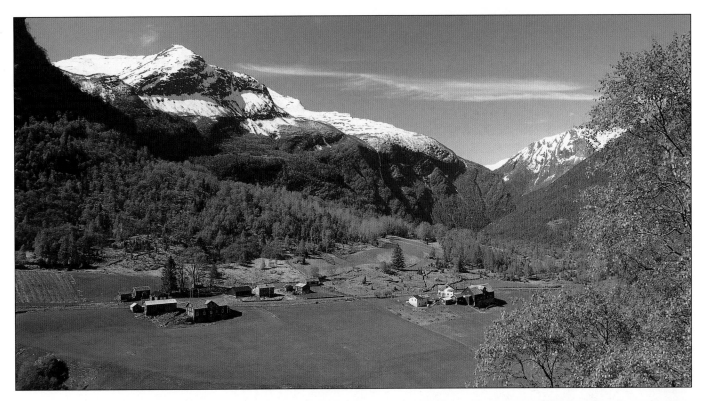

FOOD FROM UNSPOILT NATURE

Norway's coastline extends for more than 21,000 kilometres, and its seas are rich in fish. So fish has always played a central role in Norwegian cuisine.

Unspoilt Norwegian nature and the slow ripening process this far north give unrivalled flavour to fruit, berries and vegetables. The animals that graze on the succulent green grass of the mountains provide meat of outstanding quality.

OSLO AND THE OSLO FJORD

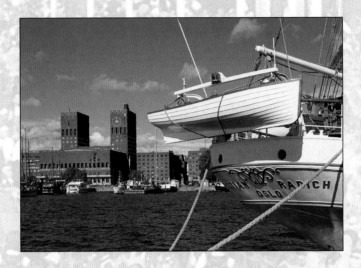

Take the sea route to Oslo. Enjoy the most beautiful seaward approach that any city could desire. Watch fertile cornfields and smooth, inviting rocks glide past as white sails welcome you to Norway's green capital at the end of the Oslo fjord. With its thousand years of history, Oslo offers a glorious intermingling of culture, entertainment and nature. Experience Norway's national day in Oslo, with the unforgettable procession of children along the street of Karl Johan. Everybody wants to see the Viking Ship Museum, the Vigeland Sculpture Park and the Holmenkollen ski jump, but don't forget to enjoy the exhilarating sea breeze and the freshly cooked shrimps at Aker Brygge on the waterfront.

Left: Norway's national day, 17 May, in Oslo.
Children's procession along the street of Karl Johan.

Above: Rådhuset (the City Hall).

OSLO

Oslo is the capital of Norway as well as its largest city, with a population of about 510,000. The Royal Palace, the Storting (parliament), the government and other central State institutions are all located here. The Vikings founded Oslo in about 1000, and it became the capital of Norway in 1299. Today, Oslo is a modern city with busy shopping districts, a wealth of cultural events and an exciting nightlife. But nature is never far away - forests and sea surround Oslo on all sides.

Above and right: Along Karl Johan - Oslo's vibrant main street - the Studenterlunden park extends like a green oasis.
Far right: Oslo Cathedral.

Above and left: The harbour fringes the bustling waterfront near Aker Brygge, Rådhuset (the City Hall) and Akershus Fortress.

Following pages: Festive fireworks above Akershus Fortress.

Vigeland Park is one of Oslo's major tourist attractions. Gustav Vigeland's extensive sculpture park is unique in the world.

The most famous sculptures are the Monolith, a granite column 17 metres high, and the bronze figure "Sinnataggen" (Boy in a Tantrum).

Many museums are gathered on Bygdøy peninsula. The Viking Ship Museum (left), the Kon-Tiki Museum (above), the Norwegian Folk Museum and the Fram Museum are the most visited attractions.

Holmenkollen (below) is Oslo's well-known ski jump and stadium. The Holmenkollen Ski Festival takes place here every year, featuring skiing events that attract enthusiastic crowds.

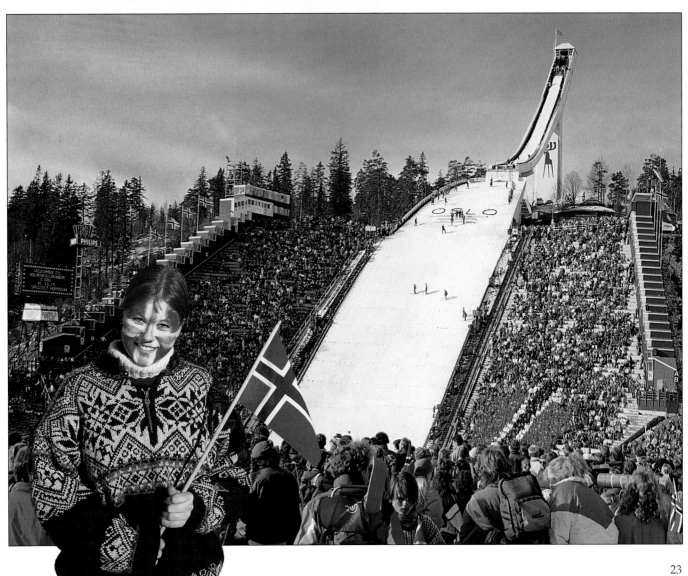

THE OSLO FJORD

The Oslo Fjord stretches from Oslo to the Færder lighthouse. This is an important transport artery, with many ferries and other ships. The fjord is also a popular recreational area, attracting thousands of pleasure craft in summer. Sailing into the Oslo Fjord, we pass many historical places: To the east is the border town of Halden with the Fredriksten fortress, and Fredrikstad with Gamlebyen, Scandinavia's best-preserved fortress town. To the west is Tønsberg, the oldest city in Norway.

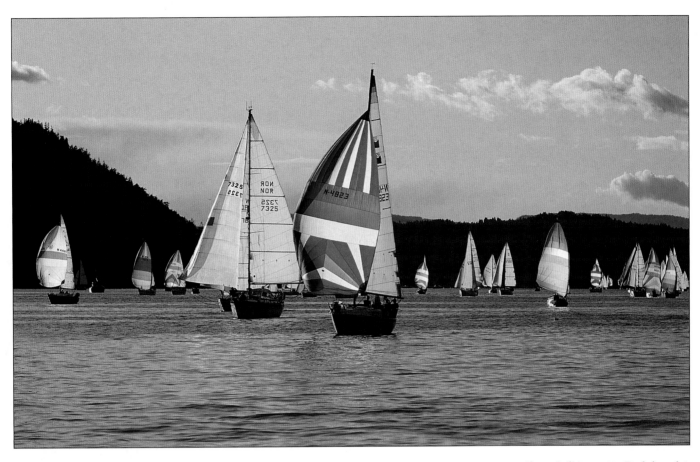

Left: Færder lighthouse.

Below: Tønsberg.

Above: Sailing regatta, Drøbaksundet.

Below: Gamlebyen (the Old Town) in Fredrikstad.

EAST NORWAY

ENDLESS MOUNTAIN PLATEAUS, DIZZYING PEAKS AND PRECIPICES, DEEP FORESTS, FERTILE VALLEYS, RIVERS AND LAKES TEEMING WITH FISH. IRRESISTIBLE CHALLENGES AWAIT SKIERS, RAMBLERS, ANGLERS, HUNTERS, AND EVERYONE ELSE WHO RELISHES FRESH, UNSPOILT NATURE. THE CULTURAL HERITAGE OF EAST NORWAY ALSO OFFERS A WEALTH OF EXCITING POSSIBILITIES. HERE YOU CAN DISCOVER GEMS OF THE COUNTRY'S UNIQUE WOODEN ARCHI-TECTURE, AND SAIL ON LAKE MJØSA ON THE WORLD'S OLDEST PADDLE STEAMER IN REGULAR SERVICE.

Left: Maihaugen Folk Museum, Lillehammer.
Above: Skibladner - "The White Swan of the Mjøsa".

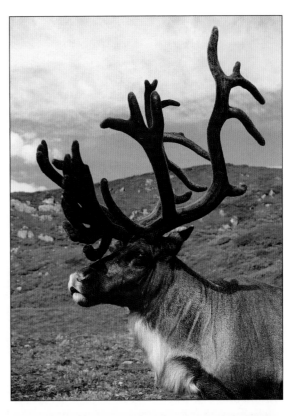

THE MOUNTAINS

Norwegians have a passion for the outdoor life. They use nature both as a sports arena and an exhilarating opportunity for recreation. For many people, the mountains hold a special attraction. They offer demanding challenges and dramatic panoramas, but also peace and harmony on the banks of a calm mountain lake.

Left: View of Gjende in the Jotunheimen.
Below left: Walking in the mountains.
Below: Autumn in Rondane.

Above: Purple mountain saxifrage and glacier crowfoot.
Right: Reindeer buck.

FOREST COUNTRY

The endless forests of East Norway - the kingdom of the elk - offer all kinds of experiences in nature. Here, there are excellent opportunities for hunting, and a wealth of forest berries and mushrooms. There are rare animals living here, such as bears, wolves, and lynxes. And those with a lively imagination might catch a glimpse of a real Norwegian troll in the depths of the forests.

Left: Brown bear.
Above left: Grouse hunt.
Above right: Mushrooms from nature's pantry.
Above, far right: Blackcock.
Right: The elk - king of the forest.

Previous pages : Winter evening in the Jotunheimen.

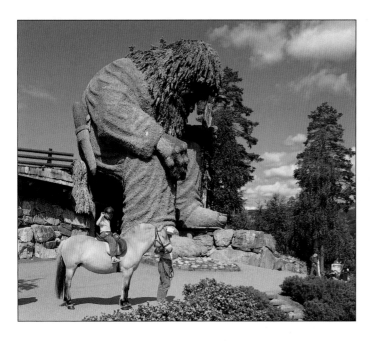

Gudbrandsdalen is the longest valley in Norway. To the
north, the valley is enclosed by the mountains of Dovre,
Rondane and Jotunheimen. Further south in the valley,
you will find a fertile agricultural area with many large
and beautiful farms. The oldest date back to Viking times.

*Above: Hunderfossen Familiepark near Lillehammer provides an
opportunity to meet many of the colourful figures from Norwegian folklore.
Here, you can also greet the world's largest troll.*

*Right: At the north of the Mjøsa is the pleasant town of Lillehammer -
where the Winter Olympics took place in 1994.*

Below: Farmlands near Tretten in Gudbrandsdalen.

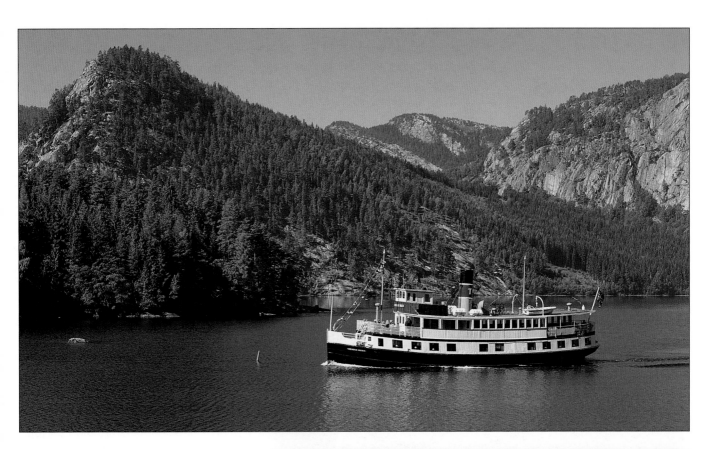

Telemark has taken good care of its cultural heritage. The old brown Telemark houses with their distinctive building style and superb ornamentation represent some of the finest examples of Norway's wooden architecture. Some of the houses that have been preserved are more than 800 years old. Traditional cultural forms such as folk music and rose painting still flourish in Telemark today.

Above: The Telemark Canal is more than a century old, and extends all the way from the coast into the mountains, ending at the foot of Hardangervidda.

Below: Rose-painted chest from Telemark.

Right: Old Telemark storehouse at Kviteseid Bygdetun.

THE SOUTH COAST

SOMEWHERE BETWEEN THE SEA AND THE SKY IN THE SOUTHERNMOST PART OF NORWAY IS THE SUMMER DREAM OF MANY NORWEGIANS: SPEND A LAZY, SUN-FILLED HOLIDAY DISCOVERING THE ISLETS OF THE SOUTH COAST. LIE ON THE DECK OF A BOAT, LISTENING TO THE LAPPING WAVES AND THE CRIES OF THE SEAGULLS AS THE IDYLLIC WHITE-PAINTED TOWNS AND INVITING BEACHES GLIDE SLOWLY PAST. ON THE QUAYSIDE, ENJOY SUN-RIPENED STRAWBERRIES AND MACKEREL FRESH FROM THE SEA, WHILE LILTING SONGS AND ACCORDION MELODIES RIPPLE OUT AMONG THE ISLETS AND REEFS, DISAPPEARING INTO THE MILD AND MYSTERIOUS NIGHT.

Left: The full-rigged ship Sørlandet near Lindesnes lighthouse.

Above: Brekkestø, between Lillesand and Kristiansand.

White-painted coastal towns lie like a string of pearls along the South Coast. These towns had their heyday at the time of the sailing ships.

Left and above: Risør - "the white town on the Skagerrak" - organizes a wooden-boat festival every year.

Above right: Lindesnes lighthouse - the southernmost point of Norway's mainland.

Right: Kardemomme by ("Cardamom Town") at Kristiansand Zoo.

Following pages : The holiday paradise of Lyngør.

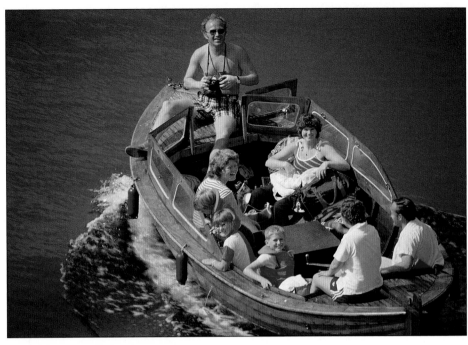

IDYLLIC ISLANDS

The South Coast is the boater's holiday paradise. Here you can enjoy the ocean, sailing and swimming on sunny summer days.

Left: Ulvøysund near Kristiansand.

WEST NORWAY

THE FJORDS OF WEST NORWAY ARE THE INTER-
NATIONAL SUPERSTARS OF THE NORWEGIAN
LANDSCAPE - ADMIRED AND MUCH VISITED BY
TRAVELLERS FROM ALL OVER THE WORLD.
WOULD YOU LIKE TO KNOW WHY? TAKE A BOAT
TRIP ON THE SOGNEFJORD OR GEIRANGER FJORD
ON A SUNNY DAY IN MAY, AS WATERFALLS, WILD
WITH THE ENERGY OF SPRING, CASCADE DOWN
STEEP MOUNTAINSIDES. DELIGHT IN THE
SPARKLING WHITE MOUNTAIN PEAKS AND
THEIR REFLECTIONS IN THE TURQUOISE
FJORD. THEN, TRAVEL TO KJERAG.
SIT ON THE EDGE OF THE CLIFF
AND - WITH INTERMINGLED JOY
AND TERROR - ENJOY THE VIEW
OF LYSE FJORD 1000 PRECIPITOUS METRES RIGHT
BELOW YOUR FEET. YOU'LL NEVER FORGET IT.

Left: The Vøringsfossen waterfall.
Above: Aurland Fjord.

The nature of Rogaland is rich in exciting contrasts.

Above: Solastranda beach near Stavanger.

Left: Hafrsfjord.

Below: The farmlands of Jæren - one of Norway's most fertile agricultural areas.

Right: Lyse Fjord and the rock formation of Kjerag.

STAVANGER

The Vågen harbour area is at the heart of Stavanger's close-knit and picturesque central area. The city is a natural starting point for boat trips on the dramatic Lyse Fjord, where the rock formations of Preikestolen (Pulpit Rock) and Kjerag are the most impressive sights.

Close to Stavanger is Jæren, with its flat, fertile farmlands and endless sandy beaches. In recent years Stavanger has grown rapidly as a result of Norway's oil operations in the North Sea.

Right: Gamle Stavanger (Old Stavanger).
Far right: Stavanger Cathedral.
Below: Evening mood on the Vågen.

Hardanger is Norway's orchard. Delectable apples, pears and cherries grow on the sunny banks of the Hardanger Fjord. Spring in Hardanger is an enchanting symphony of colour: a sea of pink apple blossom surrounded by snow-clad peaks, green meadows and blue fjords.

Left: Glacier-climbing on Folgefonna.
Right: Girl in Hardanger national costume.
Below: The idyllic Hardanger Fjord.

Bergen is blessed with plenty of rain, but the locals take a shower in good spirits.

BERGEN

Bergen is the gateway to the fjord kingdom of West Norway. The city was founded by King Olav Kyrre in 1070, and in the High Middle Ages it was Scandinavia's most important trade and shipping centre. Bergen looks out over the sea to the west. To find the soul of the city, wander alongside the old warehouses of the Bryggen overlooking the Vågen harbour. Their characteristic façade is the profile and hallmark of Bergen. These historic merchant buildings were once the centre of the Hanseatic League's substantial trade in Norway, and are listed as a Unesco World Heritage Site.

Right: The old trading district of the Bryggen.

Below left: The Fløibanen funicular.

Below centre: The "buekorps" band.

Below right: The Vågen harbour with the "Statsraad Lehmkuhl" sailing ship.

Following pages: Aerial view of Bergen.

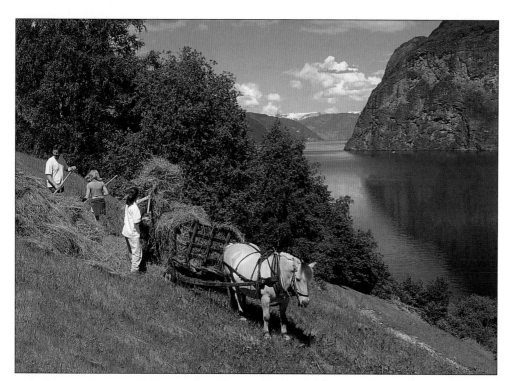

SOGN

The nature of Sogn is awe-inspiring. The Sogn Fjord is the longest fjord in the world, and Jostedalsbreen is the largest glacier on the European mainland.

Left: Mowing - the good old way.

Below: Feigumfoss near the Sogn Fjord, one of the highest waterfalls in Norway.

Right: Bergsetbreen in Jostedalen, an arm of the Jostedalsbreen glacier.

The areas near the Jostedalsbreen glacier offer fascinating contrasts. Luxuriant meadows studded with colourful flowers grow up to the edges of impressive glacier arms, and romantic clusters of summer farms are reflected in calm water surrounded by towering peaks. After a trip into the Briksdalen valley with the good-tempered and sturdy fjord horse as your patient companion, you understand why this area is one of Norway's most popular tourist destinations.

Left: The Briksdalsbreen glacier.
Below: Briksdalsfossen waterfall.

Above: Summer farms overlooking the lake of Loenvatn.
Right: Girls in national dress near the Jølstravatnet lake.
Following pages: Geiranger.

ÅLESUND

After the great fire of 1904, the town was rebuilt in the architectural style of the period - Art Nouveau inspired by the German Jugendstil movement. Ålesund is one of the few preserved Art Nouveau towns in the world. From the centre, a path leads up to the Aksla view-point. Here, you have a superb view of the town, the sea and the Sunnmøre Alps.

Above: Ålesund seen from the Aksla viewpoint.
Below: Details from the Art Nouveau architecture.

62

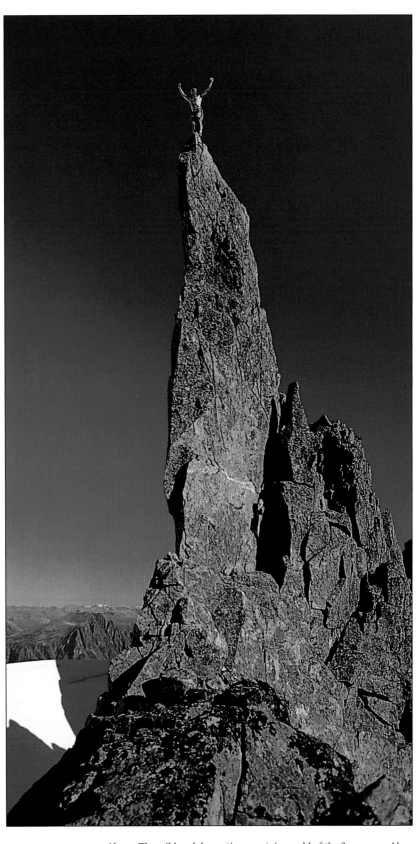

Above: The wild and dramatic mountain world of the Sunnmøre Alps.

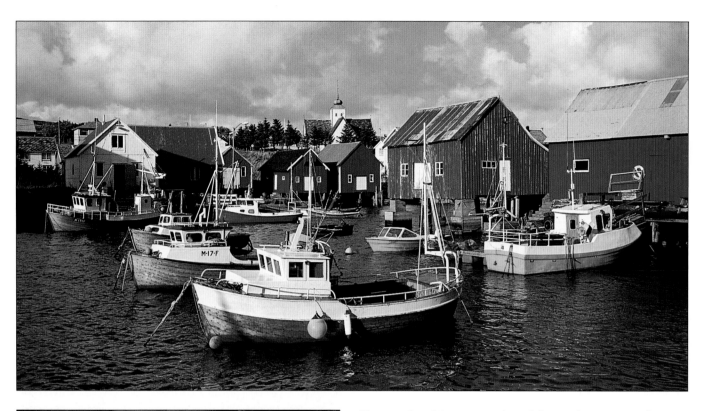

The awe-inspiring mountains of the north-west coast lure those who seek nature's exciting challenges. Trollveggen in Romsdalen with its dizzying 1000-metre precipice attracts mountain climbers from all over the world.

Above left: The fishing village of Bud on the Møre coast.
Left and below: Trollstigveien is one of the most impressive roads in Norway.
Above right: Fish bite readily, both along the coast and in the rivers.
Above, far right: Rafting.
Right: Trollveggen in Romsdalen.

CENTRAL NORWAY

Here, history lives on. The imposing tower and spire of Nidaros Cathedral soar silhouetted against Trondheim's evening sky. The sonorous tones of the bell in Scandinavia's largest medieval building ring out over Norway's first capital city. The cathedral is the most dazzling jewel in the treasure chest of Trøndelag County, but there are more riches to discover. Some of the best salmon rivers in the country wind like silver ribbons through central Norway's mild and tranquil landscape, and golden corn- fields ripple in the breeze. The Dovrefjell Massif crowns the southernmost part of the region.

Left: Salmon fishing in the Gaula river.
Above: Nidaros Cathedral.

WINTER

Winter and snow abound in
Norway. On occasion, Norwegians
think that there is more than
enough … Fine winter days tempt
many people to go skiing in the
inviting and beautiful countryside.
Skiing is Norway's national sport.

Previous pages: Musk oxen on Dovrefjell.

Above: The old mining town of Røros is a Unesco World Heritage Site.

TRONDHEIM

According to the saga writer Snorre Sturlason, King Olav Tryggvason founded the city in 997. Trondheim was the capital of the country for much of the Middle Ages, and offers a wealth of historical sights. The city has developed into one of Norway's largest university towns, and is an important centre of advanced technological research.

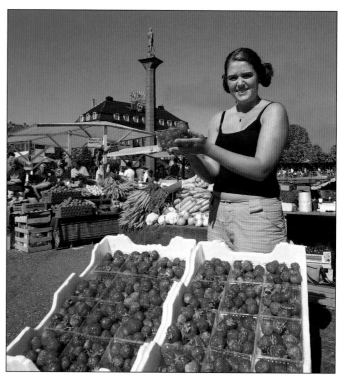

Below: The old wharves along the Nidelva river.
Above: Delectable strawberries - the sweet temptations of Trøndelag.
Above right: The market square with the statue of King Olav Tryggvason and the sundial.
Right: Gamle bybro - the old town bridge.
Bottom right: Bakklandet.

THE NIDAROS CATHEDRAL

This magnificent cathedral is Norway's national sanctuary, and the largest medieval building in Scandinavia. The church was built over the grave of the saint-king Olav Haraldson, who fell in the battle of Stiklestad on 29 July 1030. In the Middle Ages, Nidaros Cathedral was one of the four most popular destinations for pilgrimages. The others were Jerusalem, Rome, and Santiago de Compostela.

Left: Aerial view of Trondheim.   *Right and below: Nidaros Cathedral.*

NORTH NORWAY

WITH IRREPRESSIBLE OPTIMISM, NORTHERN NORWAY DEFIES THE COLD, MERCILESS ARCTIC OCEAN AND RASHLY REACHES TOWARD THE NORTH POLE. WHY DO PEOPLE LIVE HERE - SO FAR NORTH OF THE ARCTIC CIRCLE? ASK THOSE BORN HERE, AND THEY WILL DESCRIBE THE REGION WITH SPARKLING ENTHUSIASM: THIS IS AN EXCITING PLACE, RICH IN OPPORTUNITIES! A CONSTANTLY CHANGING AND FASCINATING LIGHT REVEALS A UNIQUE AND MAGNIFICENT LANDSCAPE. THE BITING SNOWSTORMS AND THE DARKNESS OF WINTER ARE FORGOTTEN WHEN SUMMER BREATHES THE GENTLE WARMTH OF THE SOUTHERLY WIND OVER FJORDS AND MOUNTAINS, AS THE MIDNIGHT SUN GLOWS OVER THE SEA.

Left: Vestvågøy in Lofoten.
Above: Cormorants in the midnight sun.

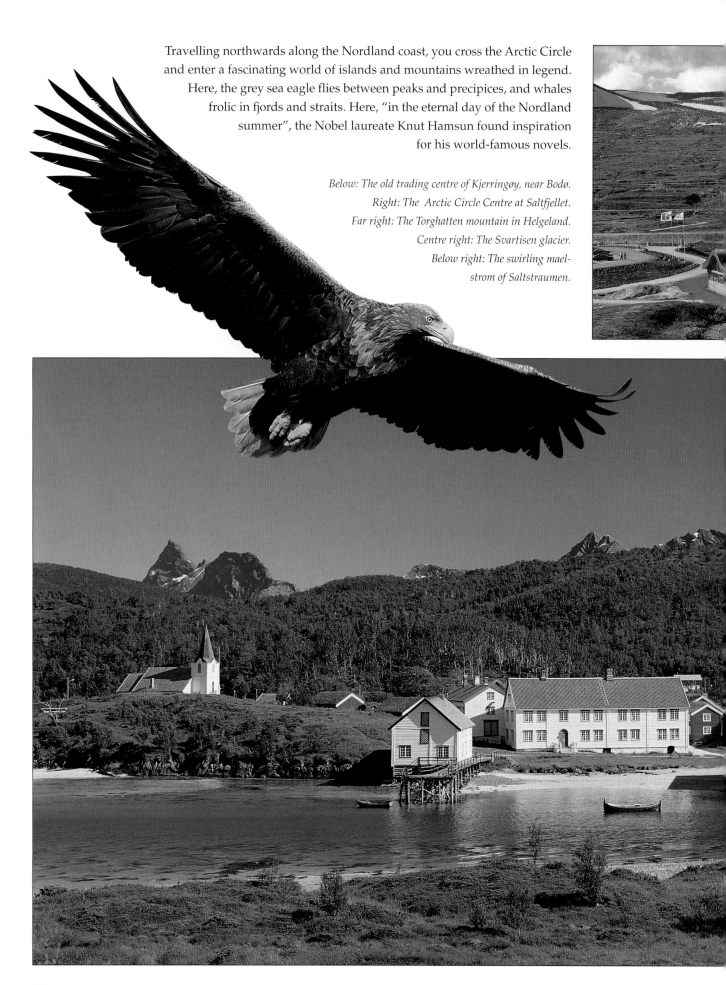

Travelling northwards along the Nordland coast, you cross the Arctic Circle and enter a fascinating world of islands and mountains wreathed in legend. Here, the grey sea eagle flies between peaks and precipices, and whales frolic in fjords and straits. Here, "in the eternal day of the Nordland summer", the Nobel laureate Knut Hamsun found inspiration for his world-famous novels.

Below: The old trading centre of Kjerringøy, near Bodø.
Right: The Arctic Circle Centre at Saltfjellet.
Far right: The Torghatten mountain in Helgeland.
Centre right: The Svartisen glacier.
Below right: The swirling mael-strom of Saltstraumen.

LOFOTEN AND VESTERÅLEN

A magical combination of steep, wild mountains plunging straight into the sea, a surprisingly temperate climate for this latitude, and idyllic panoramas make Lofoten and Vesterålen a popular destination for travellers. Many artists and photographers find this region a paradise. Since Viking times, fishermen from many parts of Norway have sailed here each winter to take part in the famous cod fishing off the coast of Lofoten. In the Middle Ages, dried fish from Lofoten was the country's most important commodity, creating the foundation for the emergence of Bergen as a city.

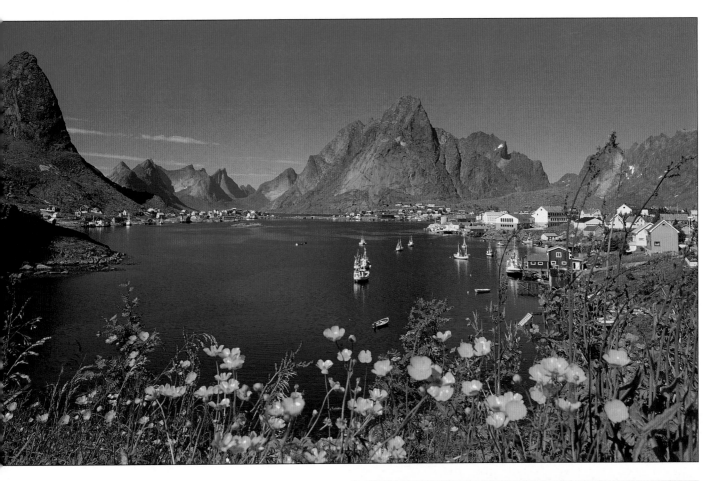

Top left: The fishing village of Å.

Bottom left: The village of Nusfjord on Flakstadøy.

Above: Reine, on the island of Moskenesøy.

Right: Svolvær, with the rock formation Svolværgeita (the goat) in the foreground.

Below: Henningsvær, with Vågakallen in the background.

Following pages: The Raftsundet channel between Lofoten and Vesterålen.

Left: The Coastal Steamer sails along the coast from Bergen to Kirkenes - here, it enters the Trollfjord in the Raftsundet channel between Lofoten and Vesterålen.

Right: The midnight sun in Senja.

Below: On a whale safari you can admire the sperm whale - a popular photo model with impressive vital statistics: 20 metres long, with a weight of 50,000 kilograms.

Bottom: The Otertind mountain in Troms.

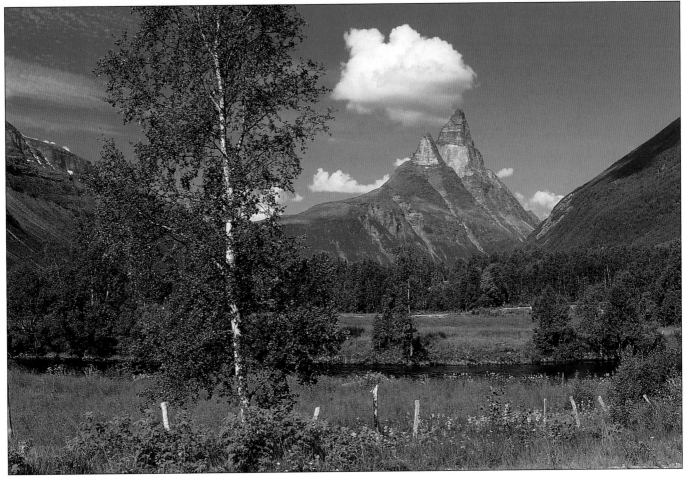

TROMSØ

Tromsø - the Gateway to the Arctic - is the largest town in North Norway. Fishing, trapping and trade formed the foundation for the city. Close to the Arctic Ocean, Tromsø was a natural starting-point for polar expeditions. The names of famous explorers such as Roald Amundsen, Fridtjof Nansen and Umerto Nobile are inextricably linked with Tromsø. The University of Tromsø is the most northerly university in the world.

Below: View of Tromsø with the Arctic Ocean Cathedral and the Tromsdalstind mountain in the background.

Right: Statue of Roald Amundsen; the Polar Museum; and the world's northernmost brewery.

Far right: The cableway, "Fjellheisen".

NORTH CAPE

"Here I am now at the North Cape, which is the outermost limit of Finnmark, and I might well say, of the whole world... My curiosity is now satisfied, and I am prepared to return ...God willing, to my own country."
Francesco Negri, 1664.

North Cape is Europe's northern spearhead. The dramatic cliff that plunges 307 metres into the Arctic Ocean is a popular tourist attraction. Each year, more than 200,000 people from all over the world visit North Cape. Most of them dream of seeing the world-famous rock in the magical light of the midnight sun. Weather permitting, you can see the midnight sun here from 14 May to 30 July.

Below: The Kirkeporten rock formation near Skarsvåg.
Right: The famous profile of Nordkapp (North Cape).
Below right: The globe on the extremity of the North Cape plateau.
Next page: Aerial view of North Cape.

The midnight sun seen from North Cape, 71°10'21"N. This panoramic view of Knivskjellodden, the Arctic Ocean and the North Cape rock shows the path of the sun from 6 p.m. to 6 a.m.

FINNMARK

Finnmark offers vast expanses of untouched nature. The Finnmarksvidda plateau is the largest continuous wilderness area in Europe. Only 75,000 people live in this region, which is considerably larger than Denmark. With their colourful costumes and rich cultural heritage, the Sami people of Finnmark represent a striking and exotic contrast to the Norwegian community. Herding reindeer was the traditional occupation of the Sami, who wandered with their animals along time-worn paths between the winter pastures of Finnmarksvidda and the summer grazing near the coast. Today, only a few Sami still make their living this way. The Sami culture has flourished in recent years.

Left: At Sautso, the river Altaelva has carved out the largest canyon in northern Europe.

SVALBARD

Eternal ice covers most of Svalbard, "the land of the cold coasts" - Norway's exotic outpost in the Arctic. This is the kingdom of the polar bear. Be warned: it may appear where you least expect it. Desolate though the nature of the Arctic may seem, it radiates an icy beauty that many people find spellbinding. Impressive mountains, fjords and glaciers make their mark on the landscape. The short, hectic summer of Svalbard conjures up flowers in glorious colours, contrasting starkly with their barren surroundings. Svalbard also offers a surprising wealth of birds and animals.

Left: Polar bear.

Above: Moss campion.

93

ARCTIC NORWAY

There are two things that everyone who has visited Longyearbyen, the main settlement of Svalbard, will remember: The stunning and distinctive landscape leaves a deep impression on you - and so does the sign warning you to beware of the polar bears. Everyone who ventures beyond the central settlements should take a firearm with them. The largest settlements after Longyearbyen are Ny-Ålesund and Barentsburg. Coal mining and trapping were the historical ways of making a living on Svalbard. The mountains still yield coal, but in recent years research

activities and tourism have become increasingly important. A small arm of the Gulf Stream keeps the west coast of Spitsbergen open for shipping during the summer. This is the most northerly ice-free coast in the world, and the northern frontier for most plant, animal and bird life on our planet. The permafrost ecology is extremely vulnerable, and demands care and consideration from the tourists who wander here. To preserve Svalbard's unique Arctic nature, 60 per cent of the archipelago is protected as national parks and nature reserves.

Above right: Sailing ship in the ice.

Above: Bearded seal; Arctic fox.

Left: Longyearbyen.

N O R W A Y

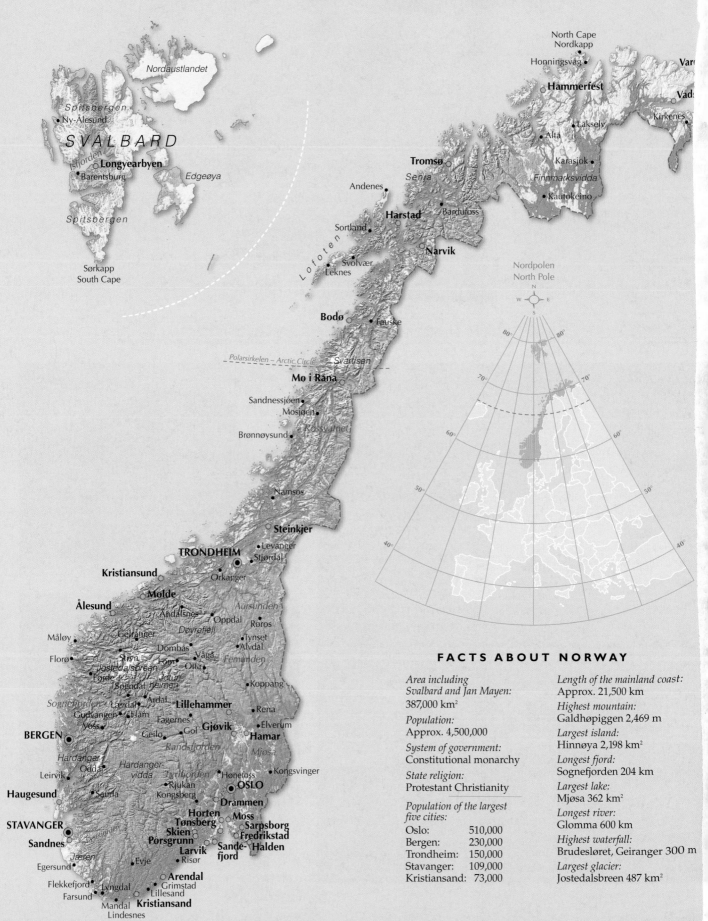

Nordaustlandet

Spitsbergen
• Ny-Ålesund

S V A L B A R D

Longyearbyen
• Barentsburg   *Edgeøya*

Spitsbergen

Sørkapp
South Cape

North Cape
Nordkapp

Honningsvåg •   **Var**

Hammerfest   **Vads**

Alta •   • Lakselv   Kirkenes •

Tromsø   • Karasjok

Senja   • Bardufoss   *Finnmarksvidda*

Andenes •   • Kautokeino

Harstad

Sortland •

Narvik

Lofoten   Svolvær •
Leknes •

Bodø   • Fauske

Nordpolen
North Pole

Polarsirkelen – Arctic Circle   *Svartisen*

Mo i Rana

Sandnessjøen •
Mosjøen •

Brønnøysund •   *Røssvatnet*

Namsos •

Steinkjer

TRONDHEIM ◉   • Levanger
               Stjørdal •
Kristiansund   • Orkanger

Molde   *Aursunden*

Ålesund   • Åndalsnes   • Oppdal   • Røros
               Dovrefjell   • Tynset

Måløy •   • Geiranger   • Dombås   • Vågå   • Alvdal
Florø •   *Jostedalsbreen*   • Lom   • Otta   *Femunden*
          • Førde   *Jotun-*   • Koppang
          Sogndal heimen

Sognefjorden   • Lærdal   • Årdal   **Lillehammer**
     Gudvangen •   • Rena
          • Flåm   • Fagernes   **Gjøvik**   • Elverum
     Voss •   • Geilo   • Gol   **Hamar**
BERGEN ◉   *Randsfjorden*
Hardanger   *Mjøsa*
     Leirvik •   *Hardanger-*   • Kongsvinger
               vidda   *Tyrifjorden*
          • Odda   • Hønefoss
Haugesund ○   • Sauda   • Rjukan   ◉ **OSLO**
               • Kongsberg
STAVANGER ◉   **Drammen**
Sandnes ●   **Horten**   **Moss**
     Jæren   **Tønsberg**   **Sarpsborg**
          • Evje   **Skien**   **Fredrikstad**
     Egersund •   • Risør   **Porsgrunn**   **Halden**
                    Larvik   **Sande-**
                              fjord
Flekkefjord •   **Arendal**
Farsund •   Lyngdal •   Grimstad
          Lillesand
     Mandal   **Kristiansand**
     Lindesnes

FACTS ABOUT NORWAY

*Area including
Svalbard and Jan Mayen:*
387,000 km²

Population:
Approx. 4,500,000

System of government:
Constitutional monarchy

State religion:
Protestant Christianity

*Population of the largest
five cities:*

Oslo:	510,000
Bergen:	230,000
Trondheim:	150,000
Stavanger:	109,000
Kristiansand:	73,000

Length of the mainland coast:
Approx. 21,500 km

Highest mountain:
Galdhøpiggen 2,469 m

Largest island:
Hinnøya 2,198 km²

Longest fjord:
Sognefjorden 204 km

Largest lake:
Mjøsa 362 km²

Longest river:
Glomma 600 km

Highest waterfall:
Brudesløret, Geiranger 300 m

Largest glacier:
Jostedalsbreen 487 km²

This book is published by
AUNE FORLAG AS
Lade Allé 63
P.O.Box 1808 Lade
N-7440 Trondheim
Telephone: +47 73 82 83 00
Telefax: +47 73 82 83 01
E-mail: firmapost@aune-forlag.no
Internet: www.aune-forlag.no

Text:
**Ole P. Rørvik and
Ole Magnus Rapp**

Design:
Trønderprofil/Asgeir Våg

Cartography, page 96:
Cartographica AS

English translation:
Margaret Forbes

Repro and printing:
Bryne Offset AS

ISBN 82-90633-73-4
Art. no. 2739

Photographs by:
Aune Forlag AS:
Ole P. Rørvik: Front cover BAE,
4BAD, 4CD, 5AE, 5BCE, 6, 8A, 8B,
9AD, 9CE, 10AD, 11CE, 13CE,
14AD, 15A, 16, 17, 18, 19, 20-21⑩, 22,
23C, 24AD, 24CD, 24C, 25CE, 37,
39A, 39BD, 42C, 43C, 45, 46A, 46C,
48, 49, 51AB, 51AE, 52CD, 52CE,
53A, 56C, 57, 58A, 59A, 62C, 64CE,
65 AD, 65C, 67, 70AE, 70CE, 72, 73,
74, 75, 79AD, 79CE, 80C, 81, 82-83,
84, 85AE, 85C, 86, 87, 88, 89, 90C, 91,
back cover AD+BA+BC+CD+CE
Kolbjørn Dekkerhus:
Front cover BAD+BCE, 2-3, 5BAE,
4CE, 12C, 13A, 38, 39C, 42AE, 59CD,
59CE, 71CE
Bjørn Østraat: 79BE

Other photographers:
Georg Bangjord: 93, 95BE
Trym Ivar Bergsmo/Samfoto: 95A
Giulio Bolognesi:
27, 34AD, 62A, 63CD
Espen Bratlie/Samfoto:
9AE, 28CD, 33AD
Svein Erik Dahl/Samfoto: 23AD
Rolf Dybvik: 36
Edvard Grieg Museum: 11CD
Per Eide/Samfoto:
14AE, 15CD, 15CE, 47, 51C,
60-61, 64CD, 65AE, 79AE,
Back cover AE+BD
Mats Forsberg/
Arctic Picture Stock: 92
Otto Frengen: 5CE
Frithjof Fure: 80AD
Svein Grønvold: 25A
GV Press: Front cover BCD
Steve Halsetrønning/Samfoto: 71AE
Willy Haraldsen: 35A
Kim Hart/Samfoto: 43AE
Asle Hjellbrekke: 58C
Johannes Haugan/Samfoto: 29AB

Husmo Foto/Kristian Hilsen: 32A
Per Jonsson: 46B
Torfinn Kjærnet: 94AE, 94C
Knudsens Fotosenter: 9BD, 52AB
Kon-Tiki Museum: 23AE
Sigmund Krøvel-Velle: 44
Øivind Leren: 90AE
Gunnar Lid/Samfoto: 77
Rune Lislerud/Samfoto: 24AE
Bård Løken/Samfoto: 28A, 29AE,
30-31, back cover AB
Torbjørn Moen: 14C, 26, 90AD
Kjell Erik Moseid: 33AE, 33C
Nationalgalleriet: 11AE
Ragnar Ness: 70AD
Rune Nilsson/Opplandsbilder: 34C
Bjørn Erik Olsen: 8C, 78AD
background picture cover
Arnfinn Pedersen/Camera:
4BC, 29C
Terje Rakke: 4AD, 7, 63E, 64A
Bjarne Riesto: 29AD
Tore Sandberg: 24BE
Scanpix: 10AE, 10BD, 10BE,
10CD, 10CE, 11BD
Hanne Strager: 85AD
Robin Strand: 52AD
Nils Sundberg: 32C
Helge Sunde/Samfoto:
53CE, 54-55, 56A
Jon Arne Sæter: 66, 78C
Øystein Søbye: 68-68, 95CE
The Image Bank/Terje Rakke: 42AD
The Image Bank: 20-21⑩
Stig Tronvold/Samfoto:
50, 51AD, 76
Arne Tønset: 70CD
Universitetets Oldsakssamling: 8CD
Tore Wuttudal: Back cover CD
Trond Aalde: 1, 34AE, 40-41
Arne Aas: 12AD, 12AE, 35CD, 35CE

Picture references: A=above, B=centre,
C=below, D=left and E=right